Striptease

Acknowledgements:

Thanks are due to the editors of the following publications, in which some of these poems have appeared: *Parents* (Enitharmon 2000), *Pitshanger Millennium Anthology*, *The Ring of Words* (Arvon Anthology 1998), *Broad Street 2* (Two Rivers Press, Reading), *Open Here* (Chiltern Open 1998), *Park and Read, Staple.*
This collection also includes some selected and edited poems from *Something Small is Missing* (Smith/Doorstop Books 1999), which was a winner in The Poetry Business Competition.

'Hinged Copper Poem Dress': after Lesley Dill's installation for 'Addressing the Century: 100 Years of Art & Fashion' at the Hayward Gallery 1998.

The quotations in the Louise Bourgeois sequence are from 'Behind the Tapestry', Mari-Laure Bernadac, for the Serpentine Gallery, London.

Cover: Oskar Schlemmer, Spiral-Figurine with Spiral Hat and Cuffs from 'The Triadic Ballet', Black Series 1922
© 2001 The Oskar Schlemmer Theatre Estate, 1-28824 Oggebbio

Special thanks to Paul Walter, for listening.

Striptease

Susan Utting

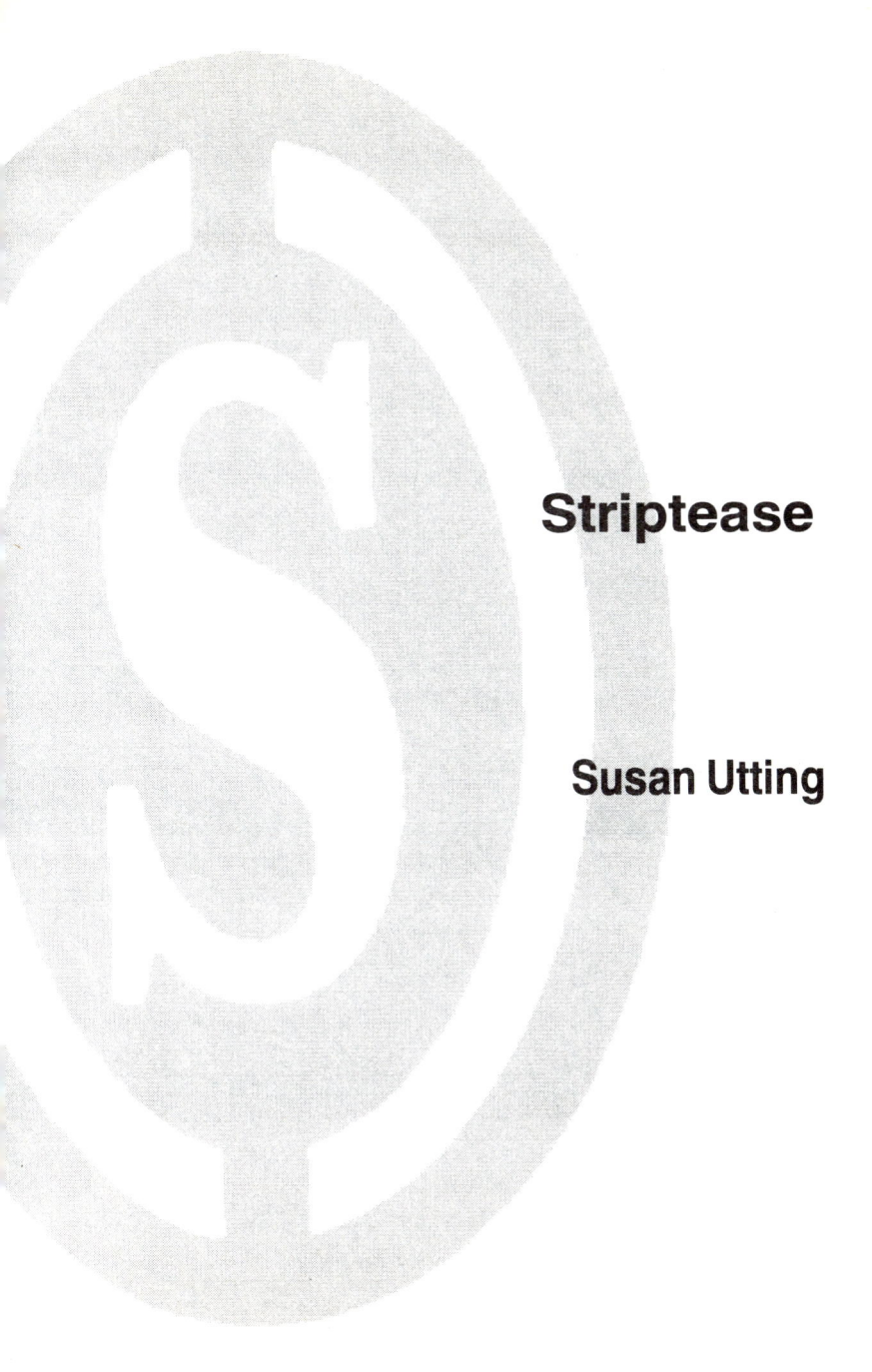

Smith/Doorstop Books

Published 2001 by
Smith/Doorstop Books
The Poetry Business
The Studio
Byram Arcade
Westgate
Huddersfield HD1 1ND

Copyright © Susan Utting 2001
All Rights Reserved

Susan Utting hereby asserts her moral right to be identified as the author of this book.

ISBN 1-902382-37-4

British Library Cataloguing-in-Publication Data. A catalogue record for this book is available from the British Library.

Typeset at The Poetry Business
Printed by Peepal Tree, Leeds

Cover: Oskar Schlemmer, Spiral-Figurine with Spiral Hat and Cuffs from 'The Triadic Ballet', Black Series 1922
© 2001 The Oskar Schlemmer Theatre Estate, 1-28824 Oggebbio

Smith/Doorstop Books are represented by Signature Book Representation Ltd, 2 Little Peter Street, Manchester M15 4PS, and distributed by Littlehampton Book Services Ltd.

The Poetry Business gratefully acknowledges the help of Kirklees Metropolitan Council and Yorkshire Arts.

CONTENTS

I THE SPOON MAKER'S DAUGHTER

8	On the Eighth Day
9	The Quiet Man
10	Flood
11	Salt
12	Such Stuff
13	Here Lies
14	The Spoon Maker's Daughter
15	A Glut of Fruit
16	Scent
17	Condensation
18	Something Small Is Missing
20	Imagine This:
21	Wonderland
22	Black Treacle
24	The Game
25	You Had To Be There
26	Understanding Angels
27	La Nostalgie
28	Night Drill

II STRIPTEASE

30	The Emperor's Last Nightingale
31	Becoming A Snake
32	Striptease
33	The Roar of the Greasepaint

34	How To Enjoy Fainting
35	For The Punters
36	The Bathers Of The Ladies' Pond
37	Sweethearts
38	Ecdysis
39	Perspective
40	The Funambulist
41	Hinged Copper Poem Dress
42	Lolita Paints Her Toenails
44	The Artist's Model Daydreams
45	Gallery
46	Spider
47	The Couple II
48	Body Language
49	Best
50	The Art of Falling
51	Orange
52	Wallpaper
53	White
54	Installation
56	The Arnolfini Marriage
57	Origami
59	A Bedsit In The Sixties
60	The Timpanist
61	Possession
62	Thin Girl On A Bicycle
63	The Florist's Assistant
64	Late

I

THE SPOON MAKER'S DAUGHTER

Yet in my lineaments they trace
Some features of my father's face.
　　　Byron, *Parisina*

On the Eighth Day

And on the eighth day
dust began to settle
and they marvelled at it,
watched it drift and pile
against the slope of walls;

they saw it profile objects,
cloud the mirrors, turn black
into grey, they saw a lacquered
box grow dull, the cuts and facets
on a crystal bowl fill up and soften.

Not knowing what to make of it,
they waited, taking pleasure in a world
grown muted, delicate and tender.

The Quiet Man

Oh yes, there were the funny turns of phrase –
like billy-o, like stink, like going like the clappers;
and anecdotes that took their time, that went all round
the candlestick, the pretty way down cul de sacs, twice
round the block and back again, and never quite remembered
where it was they'd meant to get to in the first place.

And yes, there were the words for making things,
for doing things, the hasps and offerings up, purlins,
jambs and dovetails, chamfer, flywheels and escapements,
spinnakers and burgees, jibs and slide-rule longitudes.

And then there were the quiet times, close times
for saying nothing much at all, him doing, me just
watching, holding onto something for him, steadying
a tricky bit, not really helping; like at the end of things,
him knowing how to do it right, to make it easy for me,
me just watching, holding on to him.

Flood

The lawn is a lake and still it comes down,
it lashes and sluices down gutter and glass,
the yard in an eddy of flowerheads and dross
and I am reminded of stories of sand bags
stacked on a river bank, four deep, ten high,
the unstoppable Ouse, lost fortunes and lives,
bulb fields and orchards, whole nurseries of glass
swept along, swept away in the rush to the sea.

I'm reminded of building a boat, watching
my father at work, inland and steady, doggedly
dreaming of seashores and oceans whilst making
a fresh water Fireball, his racer for reservoirs,
gravel pit Sundays, his stop gap for sea fever;
and my single-sailed dinghy, easy to handle, a Foil
for a learner, wind ignorant, nervous of water,
he made it for me *uncapsizable, safer than land.*

I'm reminded of church yards and graves,
of ashes to ashes and dust, and the waterlogged
ground, the bones of the dead in the ground,
my father there, inland and rain wet, dreaming
of salt; dreaming of floodwaters reaching his bones
sweeping them out of their grave in a river of mud,
rushing them out to the road, through the streets
and estates, past houses with lawns that are lakes,

over the common to Riverside Walk, into the Emm,
to the Loddon and on to the Thames, all the way
down to the estuary, back in a rush to the sea.

Salt

On white linen, you don't really see it,
you feel it under the flat of your finger
like grit, like sand on the beach, like even
the sharpest, finest sand, you know every grain
could be counted, that somebody, somewhere, could.

Late night at a boarding-house table Grandfather
cut next morning's grapefruit, pared the halves
with a curved knife, then sprinkled on sugar
sweeping spilt grains from the cloth with his hand
and – *waste not want not* – back into the bowl.

He poured the salt in a steady stream into cellars,
a glass row of thimblefuls, measured for morning,
then brushed what he spilt, over the table into his
cupped hand; but knowing that somebody, somewhere,
was taking account, he'd toss the devil's dust

up in the air, a curse as it went over his shoulder,
always the left, leaving a sprinkle of white at his back.

Such Stuff

I dream about journeys, unending and lost, not
knowing the landscape, the city, the landmarks
or route that I'm on, not knowing where home is –
familiar enough for a regular mover, a sisterless
fatherless shifter. But in this dream there's no one

to ask, not even the recently dead or the ancient
and long ago dead with a hint, with the knowledge,
a joke or some wisdom, a story, a spin or opinion
on where we might be.
                                      Here there are just cigarettes
offered by strangers, thoughtlessly taken, a light
that's accepted, a kick in the lungs and the heart,

that dizzying trip, familiar and heady as yesterday, after
a life time of going without, everything gone in one breath.

Here Lies

Between the A-road and the railway track
the pavement and the shingle path
the lychgate and the steeple jack
between the warning and the aftermath

Between the third month and the bedding down
the far off and the easy reach
the city and the one horse town
between the meadow and the stony beach

Between the bevel and the precipice
the splinter and the crooked stick
the bull's eye and the easy miss
between the craftsman and the crafty trick

Between the certain and the not so sure
the wisdom and the wise old fool
the toothless grin and the guffaw
between the swivel chair and birthing stool

Between the slipper and the cobbled boot
the thick of it and looking in
the body and the body suit
between the quick and dead and kith and kin

Between the A-road and the railway track
between the lychgate and the steeple jack

The Spoon Maker's Daughter

My head's too full of memories for my own good:
my father as a young man with blunt finger ends,
his forehead then as smooth as the back of a spoon,
a shaper, a burnisher, a polisher of silver,
alchemical, a turner of dull metal into spoons.

A dozen for a baptism, apostle faced and fine,
vine leaves for a wedding set, the tracery of
families, arms for the nobility, rank by serried
rank of them laid out on green baize cloth.
His hands had their measure, those blunt finger ends

perfected balances of shaft and bowl, of shoulders
engineered to last – *a lifetime thing, a spoon* –
he'd say, and show me how to see myself reflected
upside down; my father as an old man with blunt finger
ends and a head too full of memories to remember.

A Glut of Fruit

i Strawberries

Never so sweet as in June,
never so worth the wait,
the ache in your back,
stitch in your side, scorch
on the back of your neck,
the dazzle and squint –
never so flash as in June.

Never so ready to bite
never so pink on your tongue,
red at the edge of your mouth,
never the fizz, the smell, the glut,
never the hull as easy as then
as clean away from the flesh –
never so sweet as in June.

ii Damsons

So many that summer we had to dig in,
bury them fast against orchard rot,
scavenger wasps and their ilk;
so many our fingers went purple,
we grazed our arms reaching,
then screwed up our eyes at the sun
and grew swarthy and thick-skinned.

We ate till we ached, bottled, baked,
liquored and jammed; we gave them away
to the neighbours, pressed them on
anyone curious, stopping to look,
all the while thinking of winter,
waiting for frost, for a levelling fall
on the earth of those roughly dug graves.

Scent

A back street in suburban Barnes,
a stone's throw and a million miles from
Hammersmith, nineteen-sixty-something
and the smell of Apple Blossom.

Not the real thing – this was her *perfume*
and its cloy by Rubenstein was nothing like
the smell I knew: my father's trees in spring,
softer from another time, another county
worlds away from city outskirts, from a room
in a terraced house landladied by Apple Blossom.

So much of her, no hope for my own *scent,*
dabbed, as I'd been shown, on pulsepoints
wrists and nape, behind each ear, discreetly,
and so subtle, not a chance of catching here
its tingle at the back of your nose, throat,
or somewhere further in – that strange and heady
mixture on your skin of new scent and the smell
of something not quite happened yet.

Condensation

The way a bead of water stutters down a window pane
then gathers speed each time it touches other drops
until they're streaming down the glass full tilt
together in a single rivulet, reminds me of the way
a bead of water stutters down a window pane then
gathers speed each time it touches other drops
until they're streaming down the glass
full tilt together in a single rivulet.

The way my father always cried at weddings and at
everything the Queen said and when people won
big prizes on a quiz show and whenever any kind of
goal was scored by anyone on either side at any match
played anywhere, reminds me that I've never seen
my mother cry and of the way I never cry at all
at marriages or royalty, at tv jackpot winners
or at sports events unless I am reminded
of the way my father always did.

Something Small Is Missing

for afh

So you call, and even your best friend's sleeping
and you don't have a mother, or at least
not the one you need
                        right now;
even a nomad stops from time to time,
pitches a tent, hangs a hat,
                        wherever.

So you grieve, for the ones you never knew,
never even wanted – all the ones that
got away, slipped through your
                                    not fingers,
but those other small things: incompetent
thighs, or was it hearts, or was it just
                                        insouciance?

So you look, for that same old crack
bid it shine under your small door –
not in corners: you've had them up to
                                        here.
So you settle for all that Gloomy Sunday jazz
don't really know which track to go for or which line it is
                                            that's missing.

The Fancy is indeed no other than a mode of memory emancipated from the order of time and space.
    Coleridge, *Biographia Literaria*

Imagine This:

Five years old and you can plait your own hair,
sleep in a room in a bed in a row of others, nothing
midnight feast about it – imagine eyeless grubs
kept cellular and dreaming of cocoons, hankering
for the comfort of a twist of silk, not grubs
but children missing unstarched pillowslips.

Imagine this, the superstition of it:

The order of your clothing, dressing, counting
breaths held in and heartbeats, holding collars,
crossing everything for exes, fainites, paxes,
looking out for ambulances, dogs, and men with
guns round every corner, feeling in your pocket
for the string of plastic beads, and counting

beads and stairs, and cracks in pavements,
breaths held in and heartbeats, railings, footsteps,
prunestones, brushstrokes, beads on beadframes,
beads in pockets, clock-ticks, dog-barks, days till
Wednesday, bits of rubber from a plimsoll, bits of
rubber from a rubber, counting breaths held in

and heartbeats, fishbones, forkfuls, spoonfuls, lines
on paper, squares on paper, tens and units, carry one,
marks out of ten, and prayers out loud on Sundays,
Wednesday prayers inside your head and breaths held in
in bed and heartbeats, counting goes until it's your go.
And they tell you that you're loving every minute.

Imagine this: that you believe it.

Wonderland

And there I was with my un-braided hair, banded in front,
let loose at the back, pumpwater down to the waist against
taffeta blue and a muslin white sash, tied up at the back
in a bow, only that morning, pressed into pleats at the front
with a spittle-hot flat iron under a cloth, on the day of it,
socks – ankle socks, white nylon ankle socks, ballet pumps,
soft leather ballet pumps, ankle elastic and drawstrings.

There I was in a line-up with Bonnie Prince Charlie,
a robot, a fairy, a pirate, a boy in a cornflake box,
drama class cat in a leotard, pencilled-on whiskers
and mittens for paws, and my feet turned to third,
middle fingers just crooked, a dab of Blue Grass
on my wrist, my braceleted wrist, the right one,
the smell of her scent at the back of my ears.

There I was, as the line-up moved off, the parade
round the hall, moving dust on the floor of the hall
to a waltz tune, a rattling piano, pointing my feet,
toes down first to the floor, middle fingers and thumbs
holding the skirt out, Alice-blue dancer in Wonderland,
looking glass serious girl in the line with the shuffling
others, the only one keeping in time to the music
                        the only one keeping in step.

Black Treacle

Liquid licorice on thick white bread,
doorsteps of it, lashings, high with ooze,
two hands to steady it, elbows on the table
and my mother's mother letting me.

> *you spoil that child rotten,*
> *you'll ruin her*

Top of the milk straight from the bottle,
so it sticks to your teeth, tongue, top lip
all furry tashed; tomatoes with sugar on,
sucking the seeds through the sweet grains,
scraping the mixing bowl, licking the spoon
the butter knife, leaving your dinner.

> *runs rings round you,*
> *butter wouldn't melt*

And the kitchen drawer tipped out to a heaven
of string and elastic, stub-ends of sealing wax,
playing cards, blood alleys, tiger's-eyes, bobbins,
pins, scissors, a pen knife, a mustard spoon,
pipe cleaners, ringlet-rags, button hooks, matches
out of their boxes, a cough lozenge tin.

> *top brick off the chimney next,*
> *putty, round her little finger*

And her best beads round my neck for a dance
in my outdoor shoes on the polished floor,
all the better to click to her fastest piano piece –
my mother's mother letting me out to play
with no coat, in my best shoes in the dirt,
writing my name with a stick in the dirt

> *you'll have her catch her death,*
> *a rod for my back*

and bread and black treacle for tea,
with sweet tea in a kitchen cup and our elbows
out on the table, leaving the crusts, licking
our fingers then patting the plate for the crumbs.

The Game

Once, in a game of throw-me-your-face, my mother
and me, with never a word or a sound (not allowed)
with a sweep of our hands throwing smiles, throwing
frowns, throwing puzzled then pleased from one
to the other and back at the speed of the flicker
of firelight on hardly lit wintry nights – once,
when we stopped all the grimace and grinning, both
knowing the playing was over and supper-time come

she went on playing dumb, wouldn't speak but just
answered with nods of her head, with shakes
and expressions of eyebrow and shoulder, a language
of simplified party-mime signs – she went on
with the teasing, the joke of it, pulling my leg,
with her lips pressed together for silence, for minutes
too long, till the child that I was broke the rules
of the game that was ended, and ended in tears.

You Had To Be There

56 Queen Elizabeth's Road Stevenage Hertfordshire
England Great Britain Europe The Northern Hemisphere
The World The Solar System The Universe.

You had to be there, on the long walk to school
early, icy, solitary, swaddled in all sorts of wool,
nose-tip, cheek-spots red as the paint on a russian doll.

Babushka might have been the magic word, if one
were needed, but it wasn't: it was easy, then,
to dream yourself out of your skin,

make the slow shift through all those windings
out of this world and into the feeling. Feeling
like a grain of sand at the edge of the universe,

there, where a child, disembodied, could slip
through a needle's eye – easy – could spin
light as an angel's eyelash, on the head of a pin.

Understanding Angels

I have conversations in my head with angels –
the ordinary, two-winged ones, the sort

who'd be good listeners, who would take your side
against the rest and never say *tread carefully.*

The ones I choose have folded wings, a casual
grace, and as they gaze with understanding eyes

into the middle distance, they tilt their heads
a little, just as if to say *we're wise beyond*

all proverbs – we will rest here, on and off,
eternally and watch your foolishness with pleasure.

La Nostalgie

The rain was soft the soil was warm

that summer of long skirts in batiked peony
fringed and wrapped round easy hips, and shifts
of sherbet yellow, mirror sprinkled all the way from India.

The rain was soft and sweet the soil was warm and rich

when we went barefoot and patchouli oiled
to gather rain spoiled roses and the flimsied heads
of everlasting flowers, silver membranes from thin honesty.

The rain was soft and sweet and fine, the soil was warm and rich and dark

when broom pods split and rattled out their seeds
between our tattooed toes, and rowan leaves caught
in our crowns of coiled and braided hair.

The rain was soft the soil was warm, that summer of long skirts.

Night Drill

Flat on our backs on the lawn, she and I,
squinnying up at the sky, on the qui vive
for a sparkle, a glint through the cloud,
knowing the others were shut-eyed, holding
their breath, willing the doodlebug hum not to
stop, promising God the impossible, just for
the stomach-lurch single-note all-clear again;

we were the only ones there, she and I
with our eyes open wide, flat on our backs
knowing nothing of gutters – all the same,
looking up at the stars, fixing them hard
with our squinnying stare, seeing them then
as if for the first time, knowing it might be,
never quite knowing if this were the last.

II

STRIPTEASE

to go naked is the best disguise
Congreve, *The Double Dealer*

The Emperor's Last Nightingale

I'm only brown, not jewelled or mechanical,
my song is difficult, needs breath, a practised
throat, a heart that at the end of things will stop;
there is no winding key to start it off again,
no click of cog or spring, no metal teeth
against a silver drum for never changing melody.

My song is pitched according to the shift of winds
it's filtered by the summer leaves and tempered
by the winter flesh of evergreens, the ice-crack
rub of skeletons of trees. The daylight shames me,
shows how dull my feathers are – I hide in thickets
from the sun, stay quiet till dusk, then I become
a song for him, a melody, a jewel bright imagining.

Becoming A Snake

Thin-blooded since a child, I've always huddled under,
pressed myself to radiators, got scorching-close to fires
or sat back-on to the sun in magnifying windows;
but this desire to slither under rugs and coil myself
is new – the thermostats are up and I don't move until
my arms and legs are gone and I become all heavy lids
and smooth skinned body, all mind's eye, a flicking tongue,
a hypnotizing stare: I open my jaws wide at the world,
                                              invite it in,
                                                swallow it
                                                    whole.

Striptease

The glow of the tips of cigarettes through smoke,
eyes dead behind the eyes; tits, arse, smiles,
entertainment doesn't change that much –

tradition, hard times, good time girls,
feathers, slap and fishnet, sequins on
Britannia, a tableau at the end of the pier

end of an era of keeping still, lying
back and thinking of the Follies,
Moulin Rouge, The Windmill, Archie Rice.

Her mother told her once, before her
wedding night, to keep the mystery alive
keep something back, keep something on –

be slow to let things fall – slip slips
downwards. There's a joke about it:
So she kept her hat on ...

                Always wash your hands
face and moneybox, keep your knees together
getting out of cars, a glimpse of stocking still

thrills the punters, gets them going, the lads,
the saddoes, and the funny ones, the wags,
dead behind their eyes behind the glow,

through the fat ugly smoke their smiles. Naked.

The Roar of the Greasepaint

Tonight is what is called a lousy house:
        you can hear a programme drop,
a fruitdrop shed its cellophane, a throat clear
        clearer than the leading lady's spoonerism,
or the tragic hero's corpsed soliloquy.

They keep on pissing into winds they just can't
        get the drift of, improvising eyebrow moves
just for the heck of it; she checks her watch
        then exits stage left early, gets this drama
off the road in record time – curtains by 9.45 –

        they simply are not getting it tonight.

How To Enjoy Fainting

Hold your breath till the webbed wings beat
in your head, just wait for the whoosh,
stand still till you sway and your heart
starts a fat throb-throb in your ear
to a syncopated rhythm in six-eight time.

Stare back till the people flicker and glow and their
voices slow to an unwound phonograph old time low,
till they flash into blue-black one-D shapes
and their smiles get stuck like a negative film
like a photo copy when the light's got in.

Fade to black. Till the sweat stands cool
and the shivering comes and the antcrawls creep,
till you know how white you must be, impress
like a small wax girl all carefully carved
for the peepshow crowd as it bends and frowns.

For The Punters

You don't see them, only hear their clatter, mutter, snigger,
then the whoop when you come on, the urge and whistle
to *get on with it, go all the way.* And I go slowly
all the way each night, right there into the glare
of the spot, the glamour-light that turns dust into glitter.

One night I'd like to stop it there, rewind the routine music
and begin again from naked – strip my skin off, peel it down
my shoulders, arms and chest, past waist and hips, unravel it
down either leg, step out, then screw it up and fling it.

Then I'd ease off my flesh and be a bone woman,
they'd see me phosphorescent in the stagelight, dancing
like a puppet jerked on strings, and in the dumbstruck quiet
they'd hear me whistle back and laugh out loud at them.

The Bathers Of The Ladies' Pond

Each day before they slip their frocks and stockings off
and naked, slide like knives through satin water,
one by one they shake the chestnut trees and wait
for any peeping Tom or Dick to drop like plums
and scamper bruised and red-faced through
the scratching hedge or squeeze their awkward
bodies out between the fence posts and the wire.

Then all the lazy sidestroke mornings drifting into
breaststroke afternoons, the ladies of the pond take turns
to sit out on the side and listen for a rustle in the shrubs,
a crack of twig, they keep a look out for a glimpse
of collar-white or toecap-brown. Then they take up their
handbag mirrors, flash the sunlight into prying eyes till
dazzled, blinded by the glare, the guilty lookers blunder off
                                        and leg it to the heath.

Sweethearts

    the fruit of the common goose-grass

Little burrs that cling like fury to the hem of your dress;
promiscuous, they hook their small rough bodies
onto smooth silk, cheap cotton, rough wool.

Unmoved by a clothes brush,
they must be picked off, one by one
like fleas on fastidious monkeys.

And just when you think you've seen the last of them,
you'll find one more bristly rogue, snuggled up,
twisted in the fold of your sleeve.

Ecdysis

Once, in a small town in the midlands with a market place
a dance hall and a cattle market, with a Woolworths
you could meet your mates on Saturdays in, once,

in a classroom in a lunch-hour (you were skiving
from the weather) in your form-room, metal window-framed
in concrete with a flat roof that was modern then,

and set about with playing fields, with farmers' fields
and tarmac squares for crazes, proper games and dares,
for schoolbus carpark rushes, crushes, blushes, once

upon a time, and just the once – a miracle, the struggle of it
in the bottom of the matchbox you were holding in your palm
and only shaking just a little from the effort to keep still,

to hold your breath in while you watched it, saw it happen,
right in front of you, up close while you were actually
watching it, a caterpillar, tiny as a gentle, shed its skin.

Perspective

I've heard of women, wishbone thin
with starving, who will look in mirrors,
see their bodies plump as cushions,
thighs as soft as feather beds; each time
they move their skin and bone, articulate
an arm, a leg, an ankle, fleshy imitators
move in synchrony with them.

I've seen the compound eyes of flies blown up
on movie screens, the natural history of an ant
that drags a boulder sugar-grain to store against
lean winter. I've seen circus tricks performed
by giant microscopic fleas, and held my breath
to watch a toy gorilla, grown skyscraper high,
a struggling woman, shrunk to inches, in its fist.

The Funambulist

I'm blindfold on a high-wire
stretched between two mountain tops
I am a seasoned artist, skilful balancer
I know the secret's to relax and keep
the breathing sweet and easy,
let the wire take the strain.
I slide my left foot forward,
shift my weight then swing
the right one round in front,
the wire bounces at its touch then
sways a little as I inch my steady way,
one well-chalked instep at a time
towards the other side.

A score of slips and swings towards the centre
I press down with both feet on the wire and stop:
I listen to the river whisper underneath me,
hear the air that hisses from between my lips;
I raise my arms behind my head, feel
with my fingers for the blindfold's twisted silk
and loosen it until the bright bandanna falls
and brushes past my forward foot;
I don't glance down but fix my gaze toward
the mountain top a thousand steps ahead of me.
I'm un-blindfolded on a high-wire
stretched between two mountain tops,
and now I cannot move.

Hinged Copper Poem Dress

The ifs and buts of it are sharp against my shoulder blades,
at first its run-on lines strike cold against my belly,
buttocks, nipples – all the skin parts that it touches,
then the heat of circulating blood begins the chain reaction:
molecule by agitated molecule it warms to me, and one by one
the curves and hollows of its os and esses, of its bs and ys -
each letter in the mesh fills up with insulating air.

All day I'm careful, keep away from fires,
sunlight, rain; I smell its metal smell like blood,
feel tiny hinges pinch me, hear it chink each time I move;
each time I breathe words move and change their emphases,
they shift the slant of *I* and *you*, of *then* and *maybe*,
suddenly and *afterwards* – whole phrases, sentences
and stanzas realign themselves, take on new meanings.

        And when I dance its skirt
percusses to my rhythm, words fly out forced centrifugal as I spin
and spin and stop – and a caesura drops from one line to the next
and so on downwards in a domino effect, but with the sound
of loose change spilling on a flagstone floor.

When I grow tired of it, worn out with wearing I unlatch
the shoulder fastenings, slip each hasp from out its eye
and let the tinny ripple start; now there's a sound like pennies
stopping spinning in the shiver of it to my ankles, feet, the floor –
a cast off, jagged ring of words to be stepped out of, left for dead.

Free of it, I find my body's stippled inky green: a chemistry
of sweat and metal's happened, I'm covered nape to heel with
systematic smudges, hard to read; but let the focus slip a little
and there's something just decipherable – written there, against
the odds, is something like a poem.

Lolita Paints Her Toenails

Strange, pushing the soft pads in
between each toe myself, head down,
wiping the brush on the neck of the pot,
the dip and sweep from quick to tip;

strange at first that my hand shook
a little, took a little time to steady,
relax and get the knack I'd watched
and thought I'd learned.

                               But here, now,
with my knees crook'd and my head down,
my hand on the brush, the dip and sweep
and the peardrop smell as it dries –

this is as close as it gets to knowing
the strange pleasure there is in the act
that's easy now: turning nails to pearls,
to my oyster satin pink instead of his red.

All art is the same – an attempt to fill an empty space
— Samuel Beckett

The Artist's Model Daydreams
after Giacometti

My head is a spoon that dips and scoops
fine sugar from a china bowl, remembers
sherbet ochre tongues and the stain on the
tip of a finger shrivelled with sucking.

My face is a flower that turns with the sun
sneaks a look from the edge of a tarmac square,
remembers the scrape and bounce of fivestone chalks
worn smooth and round with playing.

My back is an S that aches on a stool, remembers
the scale of ascending C where thumbs go under,
the broken key and the ring of a fender, bruised
in simple time, by a poker's four-four beating.

My legs are a long case clock, a pendulum pair
that swings and remembers great aunt afternoons
the rub of a cut-moquette settee, a glimpse
of a beaded muslined jug, and ticking.

'The sculpture speaks for itself and needs no explanation. My intentions are not the subject. The object is the subject. Not a word out of me is needed.'
                                    Louise Bourgeois, 1992

Gallery

Here, I'm sidelined for looking
all skin and eye, bonesharp sensitive
to angle and the fall of light on cloth,
metal, stone,
         closer, I could slip
small as I am, through a bodkin eye,

the sliver bone that she has split
wide enough for me and her, small
as we are – no explanation, not a word
from either of us,
         we are skin and eye
and bonesharp sensitive together.

Louise Bourgeois: Recent Work

Serpentine Gallery, London, 1998-9

Spider

   (steel and mixed media)

Under her belly
    the cage of her memory
wired with mesh
    one empty chair
a fragment of tapestry

      under the mesh
        not a bone
      or a needle
        neither a spindle
      or thread

out from her belly
    the eight of them
spindle thin
    witch-fingered
clutching the cage

      the relic cell
        holding its fetishes
      keeping them safe
        close as a keepsake.

The Couple II
    (fabric and knee brace)

The fine line between embrace and clasp
is smudged, erased in one static move
into a single curve, one shape of knee
on knee, close as fingers in a clenched fist.

Look closer at the fabric – it's been made
by human fingers, stitch on stitch it's finely
knitted; there is a thread to follow through
this easy labyrinth, retrace its path until

you reach the final knot, no need to cut it,
tease it out, one gentle pull will start
the to and fro unravelling of thread,
the fine line playing through your fingers

round your winding hand, re-winding hand,
a single curve embracing, clasping air.

'My body is my sculpture'
Louise Bourgeois

Body Language

She folds her legs
underneath her, like the blades of
a Swiss army knife.

She laces her hands
like the church with no steeple,
its door tightly shut.

She keeps tight hold on
her nightmares, lest one careless
day she may need them.

She waits, and watches
dust settle, that she may write
her name more clearly.

'Bourgeois pursued her reconstruction of the past by turning to her own carefully preserved clothes ...'

Best

A pink coat with a velvet collar
double rows of covered buttons
(easy fasteners), little slits
of pockets made for sixpences
and decorated slips of paper,
talismans from Sunday School all
shiny with the magic words of Jesus.

A party frock with flounces,
champagne satin with a bodice
silver sandals with an ankle strap
a bracelet with a safety chain
engraved inside with all my names
in tiny copper plate, the date that
I was born in secret number code.

A pair of six-inch slingbacks
in blue leather (hard saved up for)
made for clicking, dodging gratings,
made for teetering up town
with mates in mohair pencil skirts,
and best, for Saturday night spinning
under hoops and can-can frou-frou.

'my early work is the fear of falling. Later on it became the art of falling. How to fall without hurting yourself. Later on it is the art of hanging in there.'
— Louise Bourgeois

The Art of Falling

I

not out or apart, not like missing
the tread of the stair, not the shock
or the trip, the undignified stumble
and bruise; not into or back on,
behind or away, not the coastal erosion
of ghost village into the sea, not like
subsidence; more like pillow-fight
feathers, like silent night snowflakes
on well settled snow, like a sycamore key
like the twizzling rabbit hole girl, like
the dream-tumble over the edge and you
find you can fly, like a parachute spider,
Peter Pan without wires on a helium trip,
like an elephant child; or like tickertape.

II

There's a knack –
you relax
as you feel
yourself go, let
yourself go
helicoidal
or foetal
a labyrinth shell
a mariner's sheet
on the deck
in the doldrums
a pennant or flag
a slippery ride
at the fairground.

Orange

The memory of orange is more neon-tangerine
than retro chic would have it; back then
it zinged, went psychedelic next to purple,
hurt your eyes like Riley's zigzags and those
op-art monochromes made cool by Quant,
Courrèges's blinding white, The Knack and
dash-bright Mondrian. And there was Marilyn
in every colour on the chart and then some,
narrowing her eyes at you, like after-image
after after-image. And now you have to stare
at the light, or knuckle rub your eyes to see
the froth and spangle turn jazz to a vision thing,
to get that dazzle, all the dayglo shimmer,
the back-then shock of flaming orange.

Wallpaper

Underneath the gold and crimson flock,
un-Julietted balconies, with vines
then a chinoiserie of junks and bridges
lovebirds, willow-blue on white, and under this
a fifties fawn and chocolate geometric.

We scrape and curl it off in concertinaed bunches
let it drop on sheeted floors and shake it off
our toecaps, hold our breath against the smell
of wetted walls, intent on getting down to plaster,
back to how it must have been for them, the ones

who chose that first time rosebud pattern, optimistic
with its spriggy stripes. And we will strip it smooth,
fill in the cracks and sand it back to basic neutral
for another start as fresh as theirs was then –
our choice, a settled snowstorm brilliant white.

White

Tulips, unexpected as a snowdrift in late Spring,
not a hint of red, not an invalid bunch – here's
only kiss-of-life pale, the incredible whiteness
of lilies, not deathly or formal but tall as a woman
painted by Hockney, white as the cat, photogenic,
full out as a single, eroticized bloom.

Then there are choirs of carnations, blizzard white,
bunching together for warmth, for the thrill of a tune
sung in unison. Soft, at the back, there is daintiness –
sprinkle of baby's-breath, lacy as love-in-a-mist, quiet
as a piano played in an intimate bar; and there at the heart,
every nuance of white in a single, astonishing rose.

Installation

After the last hushed watcher has gone,
tannoyed away through room after room
over the foyer and out through the slippery
glass that parts at the trip of a beam,

out with a whoosh to the air, to the city
at night; after they've turned their back
on the art, adjusted their gaze
re-focused for looking away;

after the last quiet guide has decamped,
quitted his post, shrugged off the daze,
the vigilant torpor, the habit of watching
both ways; after they've counted & cashed,

locked, fastened, alarmed and debunked,
after the videos darken and still, when
the spotlights and downlights click off
and the flutter of air settles down to a hum;

that's when I touch the edges of frames,
squeaking the surface of glass with my palm,
pressing myself to the cool of the walls,
inching round room after room in the dark,

feeling the friction of stone on my skin,
knowing my way like a blind man at home
to the last room – there, to the pull
at its centre of iron, cast in a sphere:

the magnificent fruit, strange, enormous,
suspended on cable, just – only just – not touching
the ground. I touch it, cold as the metal it is
I press myself to it, begin to move round, steadily

circling on through the night till I've found
that place in the heart, not looked at or seen,
there in the small space of air in the dark, in the
still, long after the last hushed watcher has gone.

The Arnolfini Marriage
Jan Van Eyck

What's to make of it – me, in my voluptuous dress,
my palm as clear as innocence, as smooth as oil
on canvas, touching his. And there are oranges,
exotic signals of fecundity, an apple, still un-bitten
and that single candle lit above his head. Above my
cast off slippers, un-ringed fingers, dream cast eyes,
there are the red and velvet draperies, the richness
of that covered, canopied in crimson bed.

There is no mystery – we're pictured back to innocence,
composed in symmetry, respectable and un-dishevelled;
truth is we were just too full of loving, much too full
of having loved each other, there, just then, and often,
to have thought what centuries would make of it.

Origami

I met a poet once, an expert
at manipulating bits of paper,
excluded (so he said) from origami classes
on grounds of obscene artistry,
in short, of phallic folding.
He'd started off content enough
with waterlilies, chinese junks
and birds of paradise with hinged
and mobile wings, but soon progressed
through natural inclination and dexterity
to towers (Eiffel, Pisa, Chesterfield)
then on to ladders that extended,
perpendicular beyond his wildest dreams.

And as his fingers learnt new ways
to crease and fold and turn and fold again,
ambition led him on till all his rows
of dancing people concertinaed out,
not hand in hand, but linked together
in erotic daisy chains, his circus horses,
plumed and prancing on hind legs, showed
perfectly aligned and detailed signs
of sexual excitation. And then the final
masterstroke that broke the tutor's
tolerance: crafted from a single A4 sheet
a moving replica (artfully enhanced)
of Rodin's 'Thinker', with a smile.

We keep passing unseen through little moments of other people's lives – Robert Pirsig

A Bedsit In The Sixties

Somebody is practising the violin
somewhere underneath me, at my shins
a gas fire pops, it scorches without warming,
on the walls the marks of strangers and their
skin cells in the air, there's an atmosphere
of gas-ring suppers and a hook where serials
of coats before my own have been hung up.

Through a window plugged with screwed up bits
of Evening News & Standard there's a view of
rooftile after rooftile over other attic windows
under chimney pots that haven't smoked for years;
below the scrape of catgut scales, a late night cab
ticks out of sync, a door slams shut, footsteps
on the stairs stop one floor down and disappear.

I rub my shins and count the seconds
till the time-switch clicks the light off
on the landing. Somewhere, underneath me,
somebody is practising the violin.

The Timpanist

His fingers drum the table, he inhales the smell
of spilt bitter as he shrinks into the after office
crush before the rush-hour-home begins – that exodus
that leaves him there, black-tied and rusty dinner-suited.

He bides his time and leaves it till the very last to drag
along the usual side-streets to an inconspicuous entry.
In, he climbs the unlit backstairs to a landing, then out into
a blinding space to find his place high at the back of things;

he hears the buzz of talk, the rustle of their music sheets,
their rattling stands, pitching strings and reedy A-notes.
He blows his fingers, shakes them loose and feels
his shoulders drop, his back relax and settle as he bends

to listen at the surface of each kettle drum, twists keys,
adjusts the parchment skins, fine tuning till he finds
the point of tension, hears the muffled throbs vibrate,
waits for the baton tap, the hush before it falls.

Possession

I've walked along his street for twenty nights, I know
the shadow that his body makes, backlit against a blind,
I imagine that same shape asleep – before I sleep
I trace it with my fingers in the empty space beside me,
say his name to warm the hollow that I keep for him.

I've watched him walk ahead of me, the measure of his stride
I have by heart, can quicken mine to his – I recognize
his footfall click on morning pavements, memorize his routes,
the way he tilts his head to hurry, every angle that his body makes,
that forward slope and crook of elbow that he keeps for me.

I've sat in cafés, been in bars at times when he'll be there,
I've touched the books he's touched in libraries and then
breathed the air he's breathed before me; I have gathered
drops of blood from my left-hand wedding finger, in all readiness
against the moment when I let them fall into the cup he drinks from.

Thin Girl On A Bicycle

I used to see her sometimes in the mornings –
I'd pull back the front room curtains, see her
peddling past, thin shinned, head down, her elbows
up like the wings on a panicked chicken; she was set
on burning calories: a teaspoonful of apricot preserve,
Pure Lemon Juice in boiled water, seven cornflakes
and a blackberry, one from the clingfilmed potful
picked from the bushes on the common, earlier.

Or sometimes, in the town in shops she'd be there
screwing up her eyes to read the tiny print on labels,
calculating in her head the value of a smear of this,
a whiff of that and always on the lookout for a life saver,
a zero rated anything, to bulk buy, stock pile, gorge on later.
And then I'd overtake her struggling up the high street slope
with supermarket carriers swaying from her handlebars,
slow-peddling in top gear up the steepest bits.

The Florist's Assistant

Each day her fingers bleed from picking thorns from
long-stemmed roses, for the sake of other people's
lovers, mothers; she takes her time to bruise and crush
the woody stalks of hothouse blooms, then strips the leaves
below the water line, takes tweezers to remove
each less than perfect petal, every bud gone blind.

For the *gone but not forgotten*, the *sadly missed,*
belov'd in this life, cherished in the next,
she stands on wet stone flags and leans her body
up against the workbench while she wires and hammers,
twists and binds, inhales chrysanthemums gone over,
day-old lilies and the fumes of waterlogged gypsophila.

Late

The long journey to town
the slow steady flow of the red
the dipped dazzle of on-coming white
and the lights against me time after time
and the stop start, stop start of the struggle to get there, soon.

And over it all a high moon
with a face-full of woe, a Wednesday
face if ever there was, scarred by the trail
of a jet, marred by the wisp of a dirty cloud,
the wink of a light in the sky not a star but the tip of a wing.

And the swift journey back,
easy and quick, after the sight
of the pair of them safe – her and her boy;
then a clear road all the way, after the touch
and the fine smell of her smell of him, over it all
a beautiful Wednesday un-clouded moon, perfect and bright,
clever and clear, as full in the eye as the look of a just born child.